Beautiful Dartm

HAYTOR ROCKS
Of all the two hundred or more tors on Dartmoor this one is the most popular. From the top of the main rockpile there is a tremendous view, which spans most of south and east Devon. On a clear day it's possible to see way out to sea, particularly in the direction of Teignmouth as the view from this elevated vantage point gazes straight down the Teign Estuary.

HAYTOR QUARRIES

There are many granite quarries near this famous tor. The stone extracted from them has been used in a great number of buildings, for example the Eddystone Lighthouse and The British Museum. Granite from this quarry was also used on part of London Bridge, now a tourist attraction in the United States of America. This quarry lies at the bottom of the slope from Haytor and provides a sheltered location for walkers on windy days. The remains of a winch for lifting granite blocks are still here.

HAYTOR GRANITE TRAMWAY

When it came to building a railroad to convey the granite down to the Bovey Basin, many hundreds of feet below and several miles from these quarries, it was decided that the cheapest and most accessible material to use was the granite itself. This unique granite tramway opened, amidst much celebration, in September 1820. However, competition from Cornish granite quarries proved too much and one by one the Dartmoor quarries closed down.

WHEAL BETSY

This is a view of Wheal Betsy, an old silver, lead, copper and arsenic mine, which once flourished here on the western side of Dartmoor. The date when it first started production is not known but it was in operation between 1806-1876. In 1967 the ruined engine house and stack were bought by the National Trust and made safe as a lasting memorial to the mining industry of the moor. It lies on the road from Okehampton to Tavistock, near the small moorland-edge village of Mary Tavy. The roadside verge is protected by a large number of upright granite stones known as 'Annie Pinkham's Men.'

GRIMSPOUND

Dartmoor is an ancient landscape formed several hundred million years ago. Man's occupation of it only goes back a matter of thousands of years when locations like Grimspound were deemed suitable places for a settlement. Here a large enclosure, or pound, was built to encircle a number of huts. The building that is a speck in the distance, just left of the centre, is the famous Warren House Inn, on the road between Postbridge and Moretonhampstead. The moors near this Bronze Age village are excellent for walking and high points like Hookney Tor, just up the slope, and seen in the photo opposite, command tremendous views over the moor.

POSTBRIDGE

This is one of Dartmoor's most popular places with the ancient stone clapper bridge over the East Dart river being the principal attraction. It is a cyclopean construction, the best example of its type on Dartmoor. The bridge needs to be several feet above the normal level of the river for very often prolonged heavy rain, on the high moors to the north, where the river has its source, causes sudden rises in its depth. Despite its strength and weight it has been damaged by floods in the past. Visitors driving on along the road towards Two Bridges may like to know that earlier this century, on this stretch of road, there was a spate of road accidents. Those fortunate to survive reported that a pair of large 'Hairy Hands' forced them off the road!

HUCCABY BRIDGE

The West Dart river rises less than three miles from its eventual partner the East Dart. This beautiful moorland river runs past the famous Wistman's Wood to flow beneath Two Bridges. This view of the river is farther downstream where its flow has been supplemented by several smaller tributaries. Less than a mile farther on from this beauty spot the West Dart merges with the East Dart at the appropriately named Dartmeet.

NEAR HOLNE BRIDGE

By the time the Dart has reached here it has become a powerful river cascading and dropping away from the open moor to enter this beautiful, wooded gorge. This photograph was taken looking upstream from Holne Bridge, a favoured location for canoeists at certain times of the year.

FINGLE BRIDGE

This is another beauty spot but this time on another of Dartmoor's many beautiful rivers, the River Teign. Fingle Bridge is on the north-eastern side of the Dartmoor National Park, about three miles downstream from Chagford. There are many fine walks leading from here. Those who like to contemplate a crystal clear river with trout breaking the surface at regular intervals will enjoy The Fisherman's Path whilst those who relish a more arduous stroll with magnificent moorland views can explore the higher Hunters' Path.

ONE SMALL STEP FOR MANKIND?

For years people have enjoyed the large open expanses of moorland for walking. There are many wonderful walks particularly in and around this north-western corner of the moor. Here we have a party of ramblers using the conveniently spaced stepping stones over the moorland Lyd below Widgery Cross on Brat Tor.

THE TAVY CLEAVE

If you were to ask most dedicated Dartmoor walkers to name their favourite valley then many would say this one. The Tavy river runs through a steep gorge, or cleave, before flowing on down past Mary Tavy, Peter Tavy and then Tavistock. It's within the Willsworthy firing range so if you plan a visit, check the times of any military firing first.

MELDON RESERVOIR – DEEP END! *This reservoir on the West Okement river, opened in the early 1970s, is located a few miles from Okehampton on the northern edge of Dartmoor.*
Today there is a large car park for visitors and some great walking to be had in its vicinity.

MELDON RESERVOIR – SHALLOW END!

One of those walks is the circumnavigation of the reservoir itself. The path on the north-west side of the reservoir presents views of Dartmoor's highest peaks – Yes Tor and High Willhays. This view was taken from the south-western end of the reservoir looking towards Corn Ridge.

BURRATOR RESERVOIR

Burrator Reservoir, on the south-western side of Dartmoor, supplies the Plymouth district with water. It was the first major reservoir to be built on Dartmoor, the River Meavy being ponded back to create this large man-made lake, which is nearly a mile long. As can be seen from this picture taken from the summit of Sheeps Tor, it is surrounded by some splendid tors. The triangular-shaped pile on the right side of the picture is Leather Tor.

BURRATOR RESERVOIR

The dam can be seen on the right. The large mound rising high on the right hand side of the picture is Sheeps Tor. Out of sight, tucked into the lower slopes of this tor, is the pretty village of Sheepstor.

VENFORD RESERVOIR

Paignton gets its water supply from this lovely reservoir, tucked cosily into the side of Holne Moor. This reservoir is sited on a small stream that runs down to join the Dart in the deep, steep Dart Gorge nearby.

BEAUTIFUL BENCH TOR

This spectacular, almost romantic, rockpile is very close to Venford Reservoir. From its lofty summit there are wonderful views across and along the gorge of the Dart, which runs hundreds of feet below.

AN EASY WALK!

Not everyone likes to scale the dizzy heights of tors that scrape the passing clouds. Some prefer gentler gradients and there is no better place on Dartmoor for a flattish stroll along an absolutely gorgeous valley than the one from Shipley Bridge, three miles to the north of South Brent, up to the Avon Dam.

AVON CALLING!

Some though don't get all the way to the dam and prefer to sit by this loveliest of Dartmoor rivers, the River Avon. This picture was taken a stone's throw from the one opposite and just a few hundred yards north of Shipley Bridge's car park. The Avon drops steeply down off the moor eventually to reach the sea close to Burgh Island in Bigbury Bay.

WIDECOMBE-IN-THE-MOOR

Most people who visit South Devon for a holiday make at least one journey to this famous moorland village. This is how it looks from one of the hillsides above. This was taken on Widecombe Fair day, an annual event that takes place on the second Tuesday of September and one that draws crowds from miles around.

WIDECOMBE-IN-THE-MOOR

Many people will have heard of this village because of the folk song that features the antics of a group of characters including Tom Pearce, Bill Brewer, Jan Stewer, Peter Gurney, Peter Davy, Dan'l Whiddon, Harry Hawk, Uncle Tom Cobleigh and all! In the song they all ride Tom Pearce's famous old grey mare. Alas the poor creature is taken sick and dies. You can see these colourful characters on the village sign that appears just to the right of the centre of the picture. Visitors like to pose by it as proof of a visit to this legendary moorland village.

LOVELY LUSTLEIGH

Dartmoor is blessed with many beautiful villages and Lustleigh is just one of them with its many picture postcard cottages. Even the pub, The Cleave, is beautiful with its whitewashed walls and thatched roof.

LUSTLEIGH *The village lies in the steep-sided valley of the Wrey. This view is taken opposite the church in the centre of the village. The cross is a memorial to the Rev Henry Tudor, once Rector of Lustleigh, who died early in the twentieth century.*

DARTMOOR PRISON

Of all the photographs in this book it's this view that most visitors are likely to have snapped for themselves, probably with members of the family in front. I hasten to add that the cows in the foreground are not my relatives though! The prison is often what most people think of when the word 'Dartmoor' is mentioned. On a day like this it does not appear to be too forbidding but in the bleak midwinter when it rains, day after day, and the place is veiled in a mantle of mist, it's the last place on earth most folk would want to be.

A DARTMOOR MEMORIAL CROSS

This memorial cross is found on Sherberton Common, close to the narrow road that runs between Corndon Tor and Yar Tor, less than a mile from Dartmeet. It was put there by the Cave-Penney family, who lived at Sherril not far away from this spot. A member of their family was killed in action during the First World War. A favourite spot of his was the rock on which this cross now stands to his memory. This view looks towards Yar Tor.

PETER TAVY

Here Mother is escorting her young ones to Peter Tavy Post Office. Could it be that she is on her way to collect the child benefit? Or could it be that they are being taken for a tasty treat having driven Mum absolutely 'quackers' all morning?

DARTMOOR'S PIXIES

You don't believe in pixies? Shame on you! These little creatures populate the moor favouring certain tors more than others. Great rockpiles like those of Sheepstor are ideal habitats for them. However Pixieland, near Dartmeet, is also a favoured spot. Here pixies of all shapes and sizes will be found.

THE WINTER MOOR

When Dartmoor is like this it's beautiful to behold. Here the conglomeration of buildings is The Powder Mills beside the road from Postbridge to Two Bridges. From 1844-1872 it was the scene of great activity with black powder (or gunpowder) being manufactured here. This industrial enterprise finished soon after the invention of dynamite but the remains of the buildings where the powder was processed are still visible.

BUCKLAND IN THE MOOR

We finish our colourful caper around Dartmoor with these much photographed cottages that have appeared on calendars, biscuit tins, tea-towels and now have won the ultimate accolade – inclusion in this book! Buckland in the Moor is located between Ashburton and Widecombe. Its other attractions include the Round House Craft Centre just along the road, The Ten Commandments carved on Buckland Beacon high above, and an unusual clock-face on the church that spells out "My Dear Mother."
We hope that you will enjoy this book and keep it as a lasting souvenir of your visit to Dartmoor. It is a beautiful place, a land of rugged rocky hills, fast flowing streams that glisten with silver in the sunshine, a moor for all seasons. Should you want to discover more of its secrets, then we have a wide range of books to complete your Dartmoor education …